TAKE YOUR POSITION

Six keys to unleashing your personal power and becoming a person of influence!

Candra Ward

Rain Publishing

KNIGHTDALE, NORTH CAROLINA

Candra Ward/Rain Publishing, LLC
PO Box 702
Knightdale, NC 27545
www.rainpublishing.com

Cover design by Trevis C. Bailey of www.SDCreativeworks.com

Ordering Information:
Quantity sales. Special discounts are available on quantity purchases by corporations, associations, and others. For details, contact the "Special Sales Department" at the address above.

Take Your Position/ Candra Ward. -- 1st ed.
ISBN 978-0-9908453-7-9

www.AskCandra.com
www.CandraWard.com
www.HairSpeaks.com

This book is dedicated to my two sons Amir and Gabriel. May every life transforming word in this book permeate through your being and come alive in your life.

CONTENTS

Master the 7 basic steps in creating your personal brand and make yourself an expert in high demand

Develop and execute the 3 P's of life skills that will help to change your life and get you to the top

Testimonials

I had the pleasure of sitting in one of Candra's seminars and it was one of the best I've ever attended. *She was clear, concise, and straight to the point. She was motivated and ready to engage with the group, and there was never a dull moment. She also interacted with us, as well as made us laugh. Having her come to your organization will be one of the best decisions you will ever make!"*

_Willandra Mcgahee, Forida Career College

Today I learned where I was falling short as far as picking up my true goals and learning the direction in which I need to go. Thank you Candra!

_Anthony McClearon, Western Illinois University

Candra really taught me to be confident as well as teaching me how to determine my purpose and passion. I need to be confident about what I am doing and know that I am able to achieve my goals.

_Jazmin Caldwell, University of Colorado

Today I feel like I gained a lot of confidence in pursuing my purpose in life as well as finding what my passion is.

_Justin Sparoll, Sam Houston University

I had the pleasure of meeting with Candra and one of the things she spoke about was living life with purpose. She inspired me because she said to do something your passionate about, no matter how much money or benefit it brings. She said once you trust God everything else will fall in place.

_Amiose Simbert, Hollywood Florida

Introduction

"Take Your Position" was exclusively designed to bring life transformation and revolutionize your thinking. This book holds 6 important keys that are imperative to study and put into action.

I believe that many people want to change but they just don't know how. I offer solutions that will guarantee your personal and professional growth if you follow them.

Statistically, ninety eight percent of the population are living mediocre lives and only two percent are living there dreams and enjoying full financial freedom.

People have been engraved with mindsets that have hindered them from moving forward and believing that they can be whatever they want to be. It almost seems like a paradox to some and far-fetched. Fortunately we have the power to change our mind in an instant. Did you know that a change of mind can transform your entire life in just a second? We are what we think, so think BIG!

While reading this book whether in a group setting or by yourself, make sure to get involved in the worksheets and activities. I created them to help you visualize where you are as well as where you want to go.

You are a wonderful creation that was born for a purpose. Your very existence is here to make world changes. Trust, Believe and Conquer!

Come on let's not waste any more time. Let's do what we were called to do!

CHAPTER ONE

Failure? Not an Option!

Understand how adversity and distraction come to knock you out of position, and what to do to regain your POWER

"Many of life's failures are people who did not realize how close they were to success when they gave up."

~ Thomas Edison ~

Failure

The state or condition of not meeting an intended objective.

Dig Deep

➢ Close your eyes and think back on three child-hood or life events that may have caused your feelings of failure in your life.

➢ Write them down on the **Thought Bubble Worksheet**.

➢ Underneath, write how you believe they had an effect on you.

(Optional) Discuss the two subjects by comparing and recognizing its effects.

1.

2.

3.

1.

2.

3.

What's Holding You?

Procrastination means to put something off. When I think of procrastination, I think of someone who feels like they have enough time to complete a project or get back to an important task when they find the time. Just know that procrastination is a sure-fire way to push you back further than where you are trying to go. It can be the number one killer of a dream. Many people have great opportunities in front of them, yet they still allow themselves to fall into that trap. There is a saying that people find time for what they want. I wholeheartedly believe that. For example, if you had a new love interest and you had to talk to them at all costs, you would find the time. Well, the same goes with your future. If there is something that you need to do that is going to move you forward for the better and it takes participation, sweat, or focus on your part, then you need to treat it like that new love interest. Don't let the right timing or your destined moment catch you off guard and unprepared!

Laziness is the resistance to work and exhibiting exertion. This is a lazy state of being. Napoleon Hill calls it drifting in his book "Outwitting the Devil." Laziness is a spirit that overtakes so much of our population. Look at how spoiled we are with so much technology now. There is even a remote control trash can that comes to you when you don't feel like getting up. Wow! How did we get to that point? I hear people say that they want that big house on the hill, and they can't wait until they get the latest car, and I am saying to myself or asking them, "Okay, that's all fine and dandy, but how in the heck are you going to get it when you are not making any moves to make it happen? It takes getting up off the couch, saying no at times to hanging out, or staying up late. Sacrifice, plus, hard work would be about right. I honestly believe that those two have become an allergic reaction to some or a transferable communicable disease. Laziness can occur with people who have been spoiled to the max growing up, and not just with material things, but with not having to do much to be an acceptable part of society in learning life skills. And, believe it or not, it can also come from the lack of exercise and eating right. When your body does not have the correct fuel, it has no charge to get up and do anything. Lastly and most importantly, it comes from having a lack of vision. People who can't see ahead gain mental and emotional fatigue and become lazy. Check yourself and see which category you fall in, if laziness has been an issue for you. I guarantee when you finish reading this book, you will not be the same.

Passivity is the condition of being inactive. The passive person has the complete opposite attributes as an aggressive person. Aggressive people don't mind confrontation. The passive person absolutely HATES it. The passive person will do their best to avoid it. They are the type of people who go over critical information via email instead of doing it face to face.

This makes it very difficult for the people in this person's life. A passive person will never answer a question directly because they fear their words will be used against them at a later time. If you attempt to confront this type of person on their behavior, they have a tendency of shutting down. Some people actually become overwhelmed enough to cry. However, their first reaction is to flee the scene. Instead of standing face-to-face with their fears and risking the uncomfortable moment of confrontation, they would rather live with it. They will suppress hurt feelings because they don't want to hurt someone else's feelings. Instead, they will only drop subtle hints at what they really want or mean. This makes it difficult on others, because they won't just come right out with it. Passive people will avoid aggressive people like the plague. They find them repulsive, rude, and abrupt. They would rather confide in an equally passive friend who never urges them to take action to improve their life. This type of person is often viewed as weak. Being a passive person isn't a bad thing. It's just different. And if you're not one, knowing how to get along with them is a skill you will have to learn in order to be productive. To understand a passive personality, you must be diligent in reading between the lines. Passive people tend to feel like a failure quickly because they don't operate in boldness.

Inconsistency is a self-contradictory proposition. Some people who struggle with inconsistent behaviors have really good intentions. They have absolutely no clue as to how they have been portraying their identity for most of their lives. It is very hard to trust inconsistent people because you never know where they are coming from. They are considered to some as being wishy-washy. There is no way to judge how they are going to react to something. You get one side of their personality which is wholeheartedly committed to doing what they said they were going to do. Then the following week, the other side of their personality changes the entire scenario because they are on to the next thing without even completing the first, or they forgot. That can be very hard for the people who are in their lives because their inconsistent behavior brings on a lack of trust. If you want to become a master of your life, you need to hone in on being a person that can be trusted with your word, and not have people on edge wondering if you are telling them the truth or not. Success does not happen to inconsistent people. And, if it magically does, then it is short lived. Inconsistency will kill whatever you are trying to do, especially if you are working hard at it. You will basically be breaking a sweat for nothing.

Fear is a feeling of dread or apprehension. Fear is definitely the number one cause of failure. Fear has killed many dreams, as well as people. If you haven't heard it before, there is a saying that says F.E.A.R. is "False Evidence Appearing Real," meaning that most of the things we fear aren't even relevant. Fear can paralyze your mind and stop you from progressing. It is a dangerous thing to encounter and allow into your space. When I think of fear, I think of a scared little child who is afraid to sleep alone because they don't want to see monsters in their closet. Well, adults are no different. Most of our adult behavior stems from our childhood. Sometimes we are so conditioned to have limited thinking that we keep ourselves locked up with the key in arms reach. It's just like a dog that has been caged up for so long. When the owner decides to finally open the cage, the dog just stays there not realizing that there is freedom on the other side. His mind has already been conditioned to that limited space. Don't allow fear to take precedence over your life and keep you from what you were created to do and be. Remember that it is a trick, so don't fall for it.

I remember a time in my life where I could not stand in front of more than one person and talk, let alone a room full of people. God has truly brought me a long way from where I was. That fear had such a grip on me that you could not tell me that I would become a teacher and a speaker.

Inferiority creates feelings of lower quality or value. Unfortunately, inferiority raises its ugly head in more than half of our population. It's beyond insecurity. Insecurity can range from mild to major. A mild case is when someone is having a bad hair day, or they wore the wrong shirt for work. That may bring on a little insecurity or un-comfortability because they don't feel to put together that day. A major case may be when a breakup occurred in a relationship or friendship, and that person starts to question themselves if they did anything wrong to cause that situation so they feel insecure. Inferiority is on a whole new level. When you feel inferior to someone or something, you feel like dirt most of the time. You feel like you amount to nothing when you are in that person's or things presence. It's as if your whole being goes downhill. Any little piece of dignity that you thought you may have had is gone. You feel like you are unimportant, your value is gone, and your presence doesn't matter. But when you are removed from that person or thing, you spring back to life. It is so sad that a numerous amount of our children and teens deal with these feelings. They try to live up to the standards of what they see in the media. When some of them feel like they don't amount to that, they commit suicide, try drugs, or fall into destructive behaviors. Adults are not exempt at all.

There are many who exhibit some of the same behaviors which is very disturbing as well.

Rejection means to discard, cast away and abandon. Rejection is very hurtful. No one likes to feel like someone doesn't want them whether it's a breakup, parent abandonment, loss of a job, turned away because of their personality and the list goes on. Rejection digs deep into the soul and causes many dysfunctional feelings. When it comes to failure, rejection can work two ways: you can become an underachiever or an overachiever, which we will talk about later on. An underachiever allows the rejection to overwhelm them and they either become despondent or get buck wild and become a person outside of who they really are. Then there are the overachievers who make it happen! They start businesses, run good homes, become strong mothers and fathers, and appear emotionally strong. But behind all of that facade, they are hurting. That strong resiliency that they seem to carry comes from their silent thoughts that say "I'm going to show them and prove them wrong!" It is very unfortunate that people go through these actions subconsciously without a clue. It's easy to mask rejection but when the negative roots are still buried vines will still continue to grow.

Self-condemnation means to pronounce judgment over oneself and declare to be unfit for use. Self-condemnation definitely is a root planted from rejection. It can come from a teacher not uplifting a student, or a parent or family member always telling a child that they are doing something wrong. People who self-condemn seem to condemn others because they think that nothing is ever right. If they make a mistake, you would think that the world is over and Jesus is coming. They never give themselves or others room for slip ups. I grew up with a very strict stepfather and he was like a drill sergeant. Nothing I did was ever right. Little did I know that the mindset he created in me followed me through adulthood. Everything had to be perfect at one point in my life. You imprison yourself when you constantly criticize yourself and question your every move. The awesome thing is that it can be changed and your internal freedom can reign.

Jealousy is fear of losing affection or position and being displaced. Jealousy is inferiority on steroids. Jealousy is a tyrant all in itself. This particular characteristic can actually be dangerous if agitated. It has its highs and lows, and when it's high, it's time to seek counseling because it can make even the strongest person act out of character. I'm sure you've watched the news when a spouse has killed the other spouse, and the family and neighbors say, "But they were such a nice person, I never knew they were capable of doing anything like that." Jealousy can make you black out. I was watching a television show one day and there were two restaurants that opened up on the same street, and were competing for business.

One of the restaurant owners allowed the competition to go too far. He felt that the other restaurant was taking all of the surrounding area's business so he decided to destroy and pour trash over the entire entrance way of the other restaurant to deter clients from going in. He then took it up a notch and started harassing the woman business owner with threats of harm. In the end, he was charged, but he could have avoided that by first practicing self-control, then by changing a few things on his menu, developing better customer service and creating an entirely different experience altogether that may have made his restaurant more desirable to the customers. In the end, he lost; he failed because he used poor morals and judgment. If you ever feel jealousy rising up, put it in check. If you feel that you need help in that area then seek it out. If you don't, it can leave you with many regrets and take you places in your life that you never expected.

Goals:

- ➢ Write a goal on the "My Goal" worksheet.

- ➢ Then write three obstacles that keep you from achieving that goal.

- ➢ Underneath that write three things that you can do to overcome those obstacles.

My Goal Worksheet

Goal...

1.

2.

3.

                    1.

                    2.

                    3.

Make it Happen!

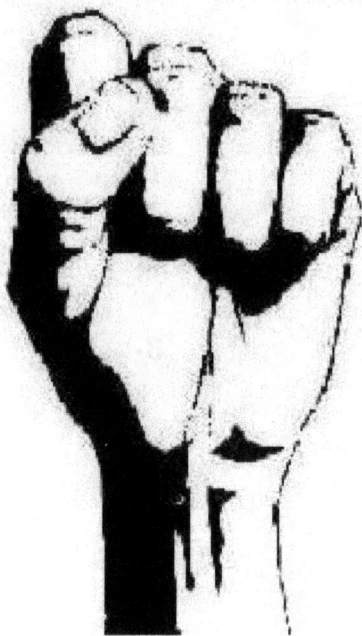

What Do I Need To Do?

Discipline is a controlled behavior resulting from self-control. Discipline can be a hard task to tackle. It takes strong desire and patience. Have you ever noticed people who say they need to lose weight and go on a diet, and do well for about a week or maybe two, and then go back to their old routine? It is a known fact that anything you do for at least 21 days consistently should become a habit. Most people that lack discipline don't even make it those 21 days, and if they do, something or someone in their old routine has the power to knock them off of their cycle if they are not strong. One way of getting help with any form of discipline is finding an accountability partner that will take on the responsibility of helping you achieve your goals. You could also create a dream board with your goals on it. Make sure you put it in plain view so you can see it every morning as soon as you wake up and right before you go to bed.

Ambition is a strong desire to achieve something. Ambition is one of those things that you see in people when they want something and are determined to get it. They are always talking about it and they keep their focus on it. They are go getters! They are always setting goals, sometimes even before they finish the previous one. Let's take a moment and visualize Tyler Perry's work, for example, as soon as he finishes a project there is another one on the rise. Once one play is out, then there is a movie following, and after that movie, here comes a TV series. Pull out that ambition in you. Go back to that dream board. Simply write your goals out in categorization so you can see them daily. You can also paste pictures on your dream board or use drawings to help you visualize your goals. The key here is to do something about it. Be excited about life. Always look forward to something that will make a difference in your life as well as someone else's. Don't just become a dreamer, but become a person of action!

Confidence is a feeling of power and to have faith in oneself. Believing in you is so important. If you don't, then no one else will. People treat you how you treat yourself. If they see that you are acting a certain way, they will treat you accordingly. I remember being walked away from in some friendships because of standards that I held, and not trying to fit in. But after a while, loneliness started to set in and doubt started creeping up. The belief I had in myself started dissipating and I questioned my friendship abilities. So after a few rounds of continuous disappointment, I began shying away from people unconsciously, and would then wonder why they would never approach me, even though I was screaming out inside for them to come and talk to me. I created my own reality and didn't realize it. Confidence is one of those things that people have to respect. As soon as I started to believe in myself and have the confidence in knowing that I am a great friend, people began to reach out to me. I walked taller, spoke bolder, and accepted who God made me. If confidence is your struggle, then one thing that will definitely bring you to that place is to start working on accepting who you are. It may not be easy at first, especially if you are used to doubting yourself, and are dealing with issues from your past. Surround yourself with people who can genuinely help boost you up. The right people can breathe life into us, if we allow them to. Trust me; if I can do it, you can too!

Persevere means to persist and remain in a task in the face of an obstacle. Obstacles are going to come, but you can overcome them with perseverance. Are you the type of person who quits? Or do you keep going? The easy way is to give up because it can be difficult to keep pushing, especially when you don't see victory in sight. Perseverance is natural in some people because they had no choice while growing up. But then there are some people that have to work at it. If you are the type of person who has to work at it, don't worry, I have a solution for you. The easiest way to gain perseverance is to pray for vision, if you don't already have one. With no vision, you cannot see ahead which ultimately leaves you batting at the wind and gives you nothing to persevere for. You also have to keep the end of your goal in mind, the way you want it to play out. Now remember, once you start on your perseverance journey every type of obstacle imaginable will come your way and try to stop you. But remember, all you have to do is see the end and know that it is attainable and you will get there if you don't give up!

Encourage yourself means to stimulate by approval or support. People are not always going to be around to hold our hands and encourage us. We will be emotionally and sometimes physically alone on several occasions in this lifetime. So what are you going to do when this happens? Are you going to run and try to find the first person who will help lick your wounds temporarily or are you going to suck it up and encourage yourself? There are times when there will be people in our lives who will encourage you but then there are those times when it is purposed for us to do it ourselves. It is needed to build character within us. You have to stand and pull your bootstraps up. Things we go through are designed to build endurance in us, and there is nothing more rewarding than to know that you do not always have to depend on a crutch to feel better, but you can find your own way out. There are two main keys that will be 100 percent effective: Prayer and faith. Knowing that you are still here and breathing means that you haven't yet experienced the magnitude of awesomeness to come. You will look back and laugh one day. Remember, this is only temporary.

Educate yourself means to stimulate or to develop mental or moral growth. People perish from the lack of knowledge! Believe that. If you do not keep yourself educated, you will always fall behind. It doesn't matter what your career is or what you would like to do, education is the key. Would you allow a hairdresser who has been in the business for years and still does old fashioned hairstyles, attends no classes and doesn't educate themselves, work on your head? Or would you want someone who stays abreast of the latest trends, so you could look fabulous? It's that simple. People don't grow because they don't take the time out to find education important. There is no excuse in this day and age because social media has taken over. You can get right on the computer and find anything you need to know without leaving the comforts of your own home. There are all sorts of websites and help out there. If having a computer is not an option, then make your way to a family member or friend's house and use theirs, or get to your local library. NO EXCUSES!

Focus means to converge on or toward a central point and keeping your eye on the prize. When you are trying to achieve something, don't take your eyes off of it, because you risk the chance of getting distracted and forgetting or pushing back what it was you were working on. Focus comes with a price. You have to give up some things and even some people for a while. We all have 24 hours in a day, but it depends on how we use it. Have you ever wondered how there could be two good students in a class and one gets an A and the other gets a C? The difference between the two is that the one that received the A focused on what she needed to do, and that was study. Outside of being naturally gifted, she had to turn down some invitations from friends and even deny herself of some of her pleasures like TV or games. Her eyes were on the prize, which was getting that A. I remember when I was a single parent and I was in my salon. I had to turn down plenty of opportunities to hang out with friends and attend weddings, birthdays, and even some church functions. I know that sounds ludicrous, but I had to stay focused because my son's tuition needed to be paid, along with all of my other bills. If I didn't work harder for that month or two, those things would have had to take a back seat until I found the time to make more money and pay them. My focus was keeping my son in his school and keeping a roof over our heads. I knew that there would be time later to have fun and get away, but at that time, I had to do what I needed to do, which was stay focused!

Characteristic of an Eagle

Possess Vitality – (reinvention, not afraid to start over, encourage self, fight). The Eagle possesses awesome and amazing leadership characteristics. I chose this one for this Chapter on failure because the Eagle is relentless. He or she does not give up! They are not afraid to rebuild if they lost everything. If the home that they took the time to build has been destroyed by a storm, they go back and start over without complaint.

Just know that there is nothing to starting over – Just Do It! All it takes is a changed mind and attitude. Change your thoughts of failure and fill your head with thoughts of success.

Practice this with every negative situation you encounter and watch things begin to turn around. Failure is a must in order to move forward.

Remember, whatever you speak and put into the atmosphere, it will come to pass, whether good or bad.

Be the Champion that you are!

Activity:

➢ Find a partner

➢ Tell each other why you feel or felt like a failure.

➢ Your partner will invent a 25-second story based on your failure in a positive manner.

➢ You will then take the 25-second story and personalize it and add the Eagle characteristic given on the previous page and rewrite the story on the worksheet, **"Affirm the Possibilities."**

➢ Now do the reverse with your partner.

➢ Discuss what you wrote and what it will take to successfully accomplish the content in these stories.

(You are speaking about each other's lives, as well as writing your vision down).

Affirm the Possibilities

My Story:

CHAPTER TWO

When Good Enough Is Not Enough

How a low self-image can prohibit you from seeing who you were created to be and what to do to defeat that mindset

"The person we be-lieve ourselves to be will always act in a manner consistent with our self-image."

~Brian Tracy~

Self-Image:

Pride in oneself, self-respect, confidence and satisfaction, and a sense of personal worth and ability.

Characteristics:

> **Low Self-Image** – Insecurity, inferiority, failure, intimidation, incompetence, fear, unstableness, jealousy, rejection, self-condemnation, confusion, lack of confidence, inadequacy.

> **Healthy Self-Image** – Confidence, belief, peaceful, successful, winner, certainty, Eagle, gratefulness, stable, healthy, unstoppable, humble.

Causes of Low Self –Esteem

Childhood Negligence is to be remiss in the care or treatment of. I have worked with plenty of troubled young people as a mentor and 90 percent of them had no stability at home. It was sad to see them crying out for attention in their destructive behaviors. I remember mentoring in one school and one of my mentees had a twin who was killed by their father. She was raped by that same man who was supposed to love and protect them. Understandably at that time, she hated men and the sight of them. I had another mentee who would always fight with her mom because her mom was all about working and partying and not paying any attention to her. So, of course, her way to get attention and cope was to fight, take drugs, drink alcohol, and be promiscuous. Unfortunately, these situations turn children into big children; they just age numerically and physically, but not mentally and emotionally. It causes them not to think much of themselves. It can turn their behavior two ways; they may not allow anyone into their space because it is too hard to trust, or they can love too hard, hoping that the person will never leave them. Both are detrimental.

Negative Experience is lacking positive or constructive features. Negative experiences happen all the time, but some can be more hurtful and harming than others. I remember growing up and hanging out with a few girlfriends who were a lighter skin complexion than myself, and when we would go places, they received all of the compliments from guys, especially, when the guys would openly say that they preferred light-skinned girls over darker ones. That was pretty hurtful and had me thinking that I was not attractive. I had never been called ugly in my life, but the rejection of not being noticed brought on low self-esteem. In my mind, I didn't feel good enough. But, thank God, as I became older, my negative experiences changed and so did my mindset. There is nothing we can do to stop negative experiences from heading our way, but we don't have to allow them into our lives. Learn how to be resilient at blocking those purpose stoppers. Rest in the fact that you have the last say as to what is going to happen.

Excessive Criticism is the act of passing severe judgment and fault-finding. Excessive criticism can cause someone to think about taking their own life or become a recluse. After constantly getting beaten down with words, and even actions, it can be a challenge to rise above. If you are consistently hearing what you do wrong and never hear what you are doing right, then it can become overwhelming. Many people who suffer with this show characteristics of outward weakness. They walk slumped instead of straight, they cannot look you in the eye, and they second-guess everything they say or do or become rebellious. For example, if a husband or wife is being criticized by their spouse on a regular basis, they are going to find someone else who makes them feel like what they are doing is right, or they are going to leave.

Achievement is something accomplished, especially by superior ability, special effort and great courage. Everyone wants to achieve great things which is just the natural order of life. But when a husband can't provide for his family or a single mother can't give her child the time they need because she is in school to make a better life for her and her child; or she has to work and drop her child off at day care, then those things can definitely cause self-esteem issues. It makes them feel helpless and hopeless at times. What about that co-worker or student who stayed up late nights working on a project only to be told that what they did was not right? That can be a heart breaker and bring on a self-defeating attitude.

Dig Deep

> Close your eyes and think about two childhood or life events that may have caused you to feel like you were not good enough.

> Write them on the **Thought Bubble Worksheet**

> Underneath, write down what you would have liked to be different about the situations.

(Optional) Discuss the two subjects so you can identify what may have caused the root of a low self-image in your life.

1.

2.

          1.

          2.

Thoughts of Someone with a Low Self-Image:

I'm not good enough
I'm unlovable
I'm unworthy
I'm not okay
Why do I feel empty?
Why do I always doubt myself?
I'm no fun
I'm too sensitive
No one wants to be around me
I am not mentally stimulating
I always second-guess myself
I hope they like me
I want to tell them no, but I don't want to look like
the party pooper
I wonder if I could ever live up to their standards

Top Signs of Low Self-Image:

Walking with head down or shoulders slumped
No eye contact
Don't accept compliments well
Always apologizing and feeling guilty
Get frustrated, impatient or angry often
Use negative, hopeless words
Always depressed
Take everything personally
Very needy
Chaotic relationships
Eating disorders
Lack of assertiveness/passive
Perfectionist
Poor boundaries
No social skills
Promiscuous
Self-sabotaging
Defensive, critical, sarcastic, aggressive
Afraid to form own opinion

The 3 Categories of a Low Self-Image:

Approval Junkie: The obsessive need for approval (Competitive, overachiever, underachiever)

Appearance: An outward show...A superficial aspect (Perfectionist, follower, promiscuous)

Apprehension: The act of seizing or capturing. (Loneliness, fearful, insecurity)

Approval Junkies:

Now, you may be the unusual individual who's untouched by praise addiction. You may savor compliments without wanting them; enjoy performing well, even if no one notices; and love working hard just for the fun of it. If so, congratulations! You have just been approved to join a small group of people that are very rare. An approval junkie will do anything in their power to be liked. These are some of the competitive people you may see at work, or at home, who will not stop exhausting themselves until they get accolades from their counterparts. It is called the Atta boy syndrome. They can become overachievers, who like to get pats on the back for everything they do. It makes them feel important. Not to sound disrespectful or degrading, but that is the same thing animals look for from their owners when they have accomplished something. Underachievement on the other hand can be linked to an approval junkie. They feel that someone is not accepting of them because they are doing too well. They will dumb themselves down by lowering their standards in fear of rejection.

Understand that the only approval you need is from God above. Some people even go as far as joining an organization to feel accepted. Now don't get me wrong, I believe that everyone has a natural desire to be accepted, but if it is in an unhealthy state, it becomes dysfunctional. They will do anything to boost their reputation within these organizations by advertising all over social media, making themselves seem bigger than they are. Now don't get me wrong, I do understand that in order to build a personal or business brand, certain things with social media and boosting your reputation is needed. But when it's done just to feel powerful, it is out of order.

Just know that you were born for a reason. The year, date, and time were set aside just for you. If you were not supposed to be here and be relevant to someone, then you would not be here. Take all of that energy that is being put into wanting to feel accepted and use it to make an actual difference in the lives of others. Remember the greatest leader is in the background making things happen without trying to be noticed. They get their joy by just knowing that they have done what was needed at the time to make a change.

Appearance

Mostly everyone likes to look good. Nice hair, jewelry, and clothes are part of their regimen. There is absolutely nothing wrong with that, if you are comfortable in your own skin. People that have to look good only for people to notice them deal with some sort of self-esteem issues. The moment they go without a stare or a compliment, they end up feeling bad about themselves, which, in turn, will cause them to try and figure out what the next hairstyle or outfit is going to be to pull that attention. You see women that cannot leave the house to pick up their mail in the mailbox without putting makeup and earrings on first.

Sometimes, when I am out and about, I come across women who can't even walk in their shoes. Or men who are trying so hard to be seen that they end up looking silly.

Some people change their personality, if they were not happy with their current one. Their walk, talk, facial expressions and entire demeanor changes. It is called an alter ego. This additional persona makes them feel powerful. It's almost in comparison to an alcoholic or someone who does drugs - they love the way it makes them feel.

Apprehension

Apprehensiveness is in the low self-esteem category. Those with low self-esteem don't like who they are, they hide behind a mask. Not a physical one, but an imaginative, self-made mask. Masks can come in the form of a fake smile, fake participation and fake business. I remember being in this category. After church let out, I would sometimes leave right away instead of fellowshipping afterwards, because I feared not having anyone to hang out with or my son and I not being invited to someone's home for dinner. So I would pretend as if we had something to do, and rush out the door. As soon as we reached home, my son would go to his room and play his video-game and I would go in my room, slide down the wall and cry until I fell asleep.

Then there are those people who are afraid of responsibility for fear of failure. It's like an employee, family member, or an organization member who turns down a great task that was offered to them that could have been of great benefit in the end. They turned it down because they didn't believe they could do it. And, as crazy as it may sound, some people are afraid of people finding interest in them because they don't want to let them down. They don't want to be responsible for their own actions.

Lastly, you have people that never have an opinion of their own. They blow whichever way the wind blows. As the Bible says, "An unstable man is unstable in all his ways. These are the people that are regularly uncertain on how to act. If they are with one group, they behave like them, if they are with another group, they mimic them. The sad part is, you never know who you may be getting from day to day.

Goals:

➢ Write a goal on the "My Goal" worksheet.

➢ Then write three obstacles that keep you from achieving that goal.

➢ Underneath that, write three things that you can do to overcome the obstacles.

My Goal Worksheet

Goal...

1.

2.

3.

        1.

        2.

        3.

Believe in You!

How do I improve my self-image?

Learn to accept yourself...All of yourself... Wake up every morning and look at yourself in the mirror and tell yourself that you do matter today. Tell yourself that you are on a mission today and nothing and no one can stop you. Tell yourself that you are beautiful or handsome, and you were created in the image and likeness of God. And lastly, I want you to decree: "I am fearfully and wonderfully made." Spend your entire day with that in the forefront of your mind every day until it becomes a natural part of you.

Renew your mind...As a man thinks, so is he... You are who you think. If you think negatively, that's who you become. If you think great, that's who you become. Believe it or not, it shows in your demeanor and appearance. It won't be hard for people to pick up on your vibes. There are going to be hundreds of negative thoughts that cross your mind daily, but it is your responsibility to quickly discard them as soon as they appear. Don't let them linger, even if they sound reasonable and feel good.

Become self-sufficient...Learn independence... Being self-sufficient is a wonderful trait to have because it gives you the freedom to get things done on your time, not someone else's. When you are constantly depending on someone else to show you how to do everything or do things for you, it can become very taxing and depressing. I have seen wives lose it when their spouses died, because the spouse did everything for them. Learn how to pay bills, sew, clean effectively, cook, drive, negotiate business, grocery shop, understand the fine print in contracts, and be self-sufficient.

Get into the company of positive people...You deserve it! Good positive faithful people are your lifeline, especially those that don't only coddle you and tell you all of the good you've done and how everything will be alright. You need honest people who speak the truth in love. These people are not always going to feel good to be around because your ego is going to kick in, when they tell you about yourself and the things you need to work on and change. But you'd better believe that they have your back.

Don't hesitate to seek help...You are not an island... Never feel like you have to handle all of your problems yourself. Understand that there are people who are willing to help you. If you don't have much family and friends to take on that task, or you just don't trust them to do it, there are hotlines, churches, and counselors, just to name a few. Don't forget that prayer is the number one answer.

Characteristic of an Eagle

High-flyer – (like-mindedness, never walk with pigeons (no complaining)

It is imperative that you walk with like-minded people, because misery loves company, like the old saying says. You have to rise above that.

Eagles have large wingspans, which gets them flying high. They are naturally very strong birds. Their talons are immensely strong for both killing and carrying prey. Their prey is always ground based. Generally, it's falcons and hawks that kill other birds on the wing, not eagles, which means they are slow flyers. The reason for their slowness is because they soar and watch thoroughly. They are confident enough to not be in a rush when they are searching for prey. They are very patient.

Just know that you should be no different than the high-flying eagle. Never be on the same level as the peers you hung out with that made you feel comfortable in your state of mediocrity.

You are a Conqueror!

Activity:

➢ Everyone will receive an index card that cannot be viewed until instructed.

➢ Each card will have the beginning of a sentence that reads "I am (ex. awesome)...because"... and you must finish the statement with a positive sentence about yourself.

➢ Everyone will take a turn.

(You have just spoken life to yourself.)

CHAPTER THREE

What Happened to Me?

Recognize how toxic relationships can keep you from your destiny and how to avoid and permanently remove them from your life

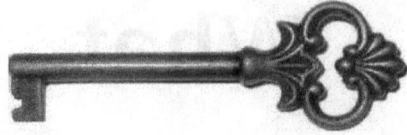

"Faithful are the wounds of a friend, but the kisses of an enemy are deceitful."

~Proverbs 27:6~

Toxic

Capable of causing injury or death/poison.

Characteristics:

- **Toxic** – insecurity, abuse of power and control, demanding, selfishness, self-centered, criticism, negativity, dishonesty, distrust, demeaning comments/attitudes and/or jealousy.

- **Healthy** – compassion, security, freedom of thinking, sharing, listening, mutual love/care, healthy debating/disagreement and respectfulness...especially when there are differences of opinion.

"Healthy relationships leave you happy and energized, whereas, toxic relationships leave you weighed down, depressed and depleted."

Dig Deep

- ➢ Close your eyes and think back on two child-hood or life events that may have caused vulnerability or pain for you.

- ➢ Write them on the **Thought Bubble Work-sheet**

- ➢ Underneath, write what you would have liked to have been different about those experiences.

(Optional) Discuss the two subjects so you can recognize what redemption you may be looking for within your toxic relationship.

1.

2.

1.

2.

Emotional Abuse

Emotional abuse affects how we feel and can distort our emotional development. Examples include Ignoring, humiliating, blaming, intimidating, put downs, no respect of feelings, jealousy, possessiveness, name calling, cheating, making you feel like you need to justify yourself, threats of no privacy. So many people suffer from emotional abuse and feel like they cannot change it or remove it from their lives.

When it comes to emotional abuse, it can sneak up on someone very subtlety. It is not bold like mental abuse, and can come from family, friends, spouses, and even associates.

Something as simple as being ignored because of something you may have done, whether by mistake or on purpose, is emotional abuse. The abuser has control and decides when they are ready to speak to you or not, while you sit there in anguish hoping that they would open up soon.

Another example is intimidation. In order to make them feel good about themselves, they will play on your weaknesses and make you feel bad by showing off something they may do better or something they may have that you don't. I had a client who had a friend who became jealous of her because she became successful in her business. The phone calls between them suddenly stopped. And when there were occasional phone calls the conversations changed. It was apparent that there was some sort of jealousy from her friend because things were just not the same anymore. Of course, that same line was used, "Oh, I've been so busy girl, that's why you haven't heard from me. The friend didn't realize she was emotionally abusing my client because of her secret jealousy, which caused my client to feel abandoned and hurt because she really valued her friendship.

These incidences will make you feel vulnerable, weak and very sensitive, and could put you on guard with the next person who enters your life.

Mental Abuse

Mental abuse is the sneakiest of them all because it involves mind games. The abuser is good with twisting everything around so they are not at fault...making you think that you're losing your mind....Her or she loves having control and manipulation.....distorting your reality...They give you false charm, tricking you to turn on friends so they can be your only friend.

I was once in a relationship that was totally influenced by mental abuse. In the beginning, it was beautiful as it always is and then about four months in, the mental abuse started. Things that we would normally laugh at together were no longer funny. There was a certain phrase I would say and that was no longer acceptable to him. He said his father would say the same thing and that would bring raw feelings to him. Then, one day, he let me use his car because it handled better in the snow than mine did. When I got home, I was supposed to call him. It was so long ago, I don't remember what for. I didn't call because I had to get my son situated and I had friends staying over. He called me and told me off sternly on the phone, then didn't speak to me that entire week, not even in church. The crazy part was I woke up one morning, around five because I heard someone shoveling snow. I never looked out of the window because I figured that it was someone in the neighborhood. When I went out to take my son to school, my entire walkway and the front of my house and my car was shoveled and wiped down clean. I ended up finding out that it was him. It was so awkward to me that he was not speaking to me, yet took the time to make sure my needs were met. That was total mental abuse because it had me confused. As I matured and time passed, I had a better understanding of why people do what they do. While I was with him, I totally lost myself, because I allowed this behavior to continue and consume me when I thought I was stronger than that.

Pay attention to the consistency of the person in your life and their habits. If things don't sit right in your spirit, then most times your intuition is correct. Follow it!

Physical Abuse

Physical abuse involves different forms of abuse. Invading your space, violence, pushing, pinching, head mugging, holding down, slapping, tripping, kicking, punching, choking, blocking the doorway if you're trying to leave, grabbing, pointing and touching, poking, punching walls, doors, etc., are all forms of physical abuse. No one starts off hitting when you first meet them. In the beginning, they are the sweetest person ever. That's what drew you to them in the first place. Then after comfortability sets in the relationship, little signs start to appear. That will last for a while, but by that time, you are already sucked in to that person's on-and-off charm, false caring and protection.

Then, tension will start building, especially over money, kids, family, the house, chores, etc... After that, the relationship reaches a boiling point and the violence begins. There is something called the honeymoon stage where the abuser feels bad about his or her actions and does everything to try to make things right. This makes the victim feel confused at first, but the heart softens up like it was in the beginning, and they feel even closer. That is, until the next offense occurs.

I had a client years ago who lived around the corner from the salon I worked in. She had a boyfriend who was 25 years her senior who gave her the world. She had furs, diamonds, a mortgage-free house, and didn't have to work. But she had to sacrifice to have those things by getting physically abused. I remember sitting in the shop one day and she ran in. When she came through the door, her right eye was shut and it was black and purple. She was crying hysterically, and all I could do was comfort her and ask if she wanted to press charges. When she said no, I was shocked, but soon realized that she was too afraid of him to press charges. Additionally, she was so mentally abused that he had her thinking that she needed him. That was the day that initiated my passion in wanting to help as many women as I could. It really opened my eyes of understanding to why people allow what they allow into their lives. What consumes your mind.... controls your life?

Don't allow your future to be ripped away by someone who doesn't even have a future for themselves. Remember, they are behaving that way because they are searching too.

Goals:

➢ Write a goal on the "My Goal" worksheet.

➢ Then write three obstacles that keep you from achieving it.

➢ Underneath that, write three things that you can do to overcome the obstacles.

My Goal Worksheet

Goal...

1.

2.

3.

                        1.

                        2.

                        3.

Breaking the Cycle!

What Do I Need to Do?

Get out of denial/acceptance...accept things as they are and cut your losses. It doesn't matter what type of relationship it is, you cannot allow it to continue to poison you. Sometimes we allow ourselves to stay in denial, because we want to hold on. Sometimes we look at life through rose-colored glasses. The thing is, many times it is false denial that we are experiencing. Deep down inside, we already know what to do. But the pain is so great, that we talk ourselves into denial and then live in fairy land, because, at least if I stay, I won't have to start over and be out of my comfort zone.

Hobbies and Interests/Get Busy... Think of something you enjoy doing and go for it. If you want to be adventurous, try something out that you haven't done before. Once you start getting out, you will enjoy yourself. You will be open and available to meeting new people and broadening your horizons.

Inform someone you trust... If it is a case where you are being abused, you need to talk to someone immediately. I know that it can be fearful, but trust me, if you speak out, you will feel so free. Pray and seek security. You can go to a church, family member, friends, a co-worker, police, call a hotline...just make sure someone knows. From there, proper actions will be taken to protect you.

Address the behavior when it comes -use "I" statements instead of "You" statements as much as possible to reduce the other persons' defensive reaction. For example, "I feel like..." "I'd like it if you..."

Surround yourself with positive people and detach yourself from the dysfunction. Believe that you deserve to be treated with respect, love and compassion. It's time to accept that you have outgrown this friendship; you have tried more than enough. Detaching yourself is the healthiest thing to do. Be courageous; delete their details from your life. Remove them from your cell phone, Facebook and any other social media site that you two have contact on. Leave your guilt aside. Respect yourself enough to want better in your surroundings. If a girlfriend is hating on you because of her own insecurities, let her go. Two more friends who are worthy of your friendship will come.

Forgive them and move on... Forgiveness is a hard thing to do when someone hurts you, but it must be done. Especially if you want to be free in your mind. Remember, if you don't forgive, you are not punishing the person, you are punishing yourself. Forgiving them doesn't mean that you will forget. But you know that you have forgiven them, if that person walked in the room, where you are and you don't have any ill feelings towards them. Now, you have the victory!

Characteristic of an Eagle

Never eat dead meat – (leadership, not settling for less)

Hang around world changers. An eagle never eats dead meat because it doesn't scavenge. It only eats the meat from the prey that it kills. Eagles eat raw and fresh meat. What a great act of true leadership. You become the leader that you were created to be. Many times, we succumb to these behaviors in others because we are lacking something within ourselves. Cripple begets cripple. Let's turn it around for a moment; some of us have actually been the abusers. But, keep one thing in mind, you can change.

Take pointers from the eagle and learn its flow in life. It would be of great benefit to you.

Don't settle for less.

Activity

➢ Get into groups of three (1 ticket per group) (5 min total for activity)

➢ The matching numbered ticket will be called (1 winning group out of the three). If time permits, you can do all three groups)

➢ Your group will blindly choose index cards with one of the toxic words on it... emotional, mental, or physical.

➢ Your group will come to the front of the room and role play an activity called "**Decisions**," which involves a toxic friend, healthy friend, and a decision maker.

➢ The decision maker will face the toxic friend and the healthy friend.

➢ The toxic friend will create a brief scenario from the word on the card and treat the decision maker negatively, according to the toxic word on the front of their index card.

➢ The healthy friend will follow behind the toxic friend once they are done and turn that same scenario into a positive one.

Chapter Four

Prepared for Passion

Take action by positioning yourself with power and tapping into your passion to make your purpose a reality

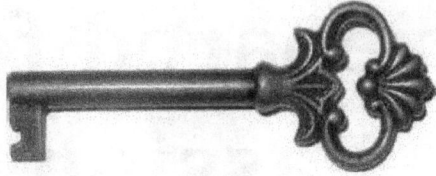

"Some dream of worthy accomplish-ments while others stay awake to do them."

~Myles Monroe~

Passion:

A powerful emotion, boundless enthusiasm.

Purpose:

An intended or desired result.

Dig Deep

➢ Close your eyes and think back to your childhood and imagine three things that you enjoyed doing.

➢ Write the three things down on the **Thought Bubble Worksheet**

➢ What would you do right now if you knew you wouldn't fail, and money was no barrier?

➢ Write your answer underneath your three childhood things.

(Optional) Discuss the two subjects by comparing and recognizing a possible passion.

1.

2.

3.

        1.

        2.

        3.

What's Stopping You?

Distraction is something that serves as a diversion or draws away from not completing a task. Society offers so much distraction when it comes to social media. If not used correctly it can pull you away from the things you are supposed to accomplish. If used correctly it can work to your advantage. Another distraction is just plain old life situations. Distraction is a problem that separates successful people from unsuccessful people. When you are focused on something, especially if it is going to benefit you for the now and the future, you can't allow any form of it to infiltrate its way in and deter you. Now the funny thing is, distraction can actually be a good thing. If it is in your life's plan to achieve a certain task and you are caught up with things that serve no purpose in your life or either the season is over, then it is good for a form of distraction to come and rescue you. For example; I was employed at a college as a cosmetology instructor after I moved on from salon ownership of ten years. While employed at the school, I found myself getting a little comfortable because I had a steady paycheck and I enjoyed the routine. Then, when I was six months pregnant with my second son, out of nowhere, I was fired. Truthfully, I wasn't devastated; it just took me by surprise. After my students followed me out of the school crying saying they planned to boycott the person who fired me, I told them to relax and that everything would be okay. I had no feelings of failure, but determination kicked right in. It brought on more motivation to complete the book that I had been slowly working on because the time and the task that were required of me at my workplace did not allow me much time to work on it. A few months of being home, I finished not only one book but two. There is always a plan for us, but we just have to let go and follow it. My advice to you is to pay attention to the distractions that come your way and be discerning of which road to take.

Adversity is a state of hardship or affliction. Most times, adversity comes in the form of obstacles. As I mentioned earlier, obstacles will always try and come your way, but it is up to you how you deal with them. Whenever you start working on your passion, don't think everything is going to be smooth – that is so unrealistic. Adversity comes with the territory. You should actually be thankful for it, because if you are a tenacious person, adversity will make you push even harder. Sometimes we can get super lax if everything is going as planned with no interruptions. Adversity sounds so hardcore, but it can actually be the little things, like mosquitos that sneak up on you and bite you. Once you feel the pinch they are gone and here comes the itching.

I remember years ago, I did a photo shoot with one of my friends and we had six models. She did the makeup and I did the hair. I had a collection of wigs that I made to display in my salon as well as for moments like the photo shoot. I had about a thousand dollars' worth of products, including 12 good quality, heavy duty mannequin heads delivered to the shooting location. After the photo shoot, I placed the wigs and mannequin heads in the closest thing I could find to transport them home, a large plastic trash bag. I got home late and left them in my trunk. When I went into the shop the next day, I took the bag out of my trunk and sat it in the middle of the shop floor. Well, it happened to be trash day. My son was at the shop that day and I asked him to take the trash out while I was occupied doing something. Little did I know, he thought my bag of wigs was trash. I felt sick when I found out they were gone, because I had worked so hard to create that collection. And those wigs were amazing. It took me a minute to suck that one up, but I did. But I didn't allow that to stop me. I owned my grief and I kept moving. I could have allowed that small adversity to make me feel defeated because my money makers were gone, but I just went on to create more wigs.

Impatient means the lack of patience; not accepting delay, opposition, restless in desire or expectation and eagerly desirous. It can be very frustrating when others say, "Be patient it's going to happen!" when you are really excited and motivated to get your dreams and passion moving." But trust me, they are absolutely on target. Being patient doesn't mean to stop doing what you are doing; it is just simply saying not to work out of timing. Some-times people can get so gung-ho on what they are doing, that they try to rush it through and put it out. Sometimes the kinks aren't worked through yet, and we present an incomplete project. Patience is a vir-tue. That means that self-control should be in order, even when your life seems to be running 200 miles an hour. Patience can also keep you from partnering with the wrong people. It will give you time to have discernment, instead of following every good-look-ing opportunity that comes along.

Pessimistic is the tendency to expect the worst and see the worst in all things. This is a definite dream killer. You may wonder how pessimistic people even have dreams to go after, and actually try and go after them. It's hard to visualize because they are always so negative. But they are people too; they just suffer with the negative syndrome. These are people that are so hard to convince. It's difficult telling them that everything will be okay. Their faith is very shallow, and, in most cases, if an opportunity presents itself, they would find some kind of excuse to uncon-sciously dispose of it. In many cases, this is learned behavior from childhood. And in other cases, this is just a personality trait that has to be worked on piece by piece. This doesn't mean that they are bad people; there are just particular ways in dealing with this type of personality. When they are around optimistic people, it can turn them in one of two ways: They can admire the positivity and want change for them-selves, or they can look at the optimistic person like they are crazy and doubt everything they are about. For example: The Optimist may say something as simple as this, "I am so excited because this project is going to be a success." The pessimist will respond by saying, "Yeah, but what happens if it doesn't? That means we are going to have to start all over." They already spoke defeat before the project was even completed. In most cases of a pessimistic per-son, it's the fear of success. Keep in mind that anyone can change; it is just going to take a lot of hard work and effort and most importantly, a change of mind.

Goals:

> Write a goal on the "My Goal" worksheet.

> Then write three obstacles that keep you from achieving the goal.

> Underneath that, write three things that you can do to overcome the obstacles.

My Goal Worksheet

Goal...

1.

2.

3.

        1.

        2.

        3.

Make it happen!

What Do I Need to Do?

Take Risk (an action that someone takes when they expose themselves to loss or injury in the hopes of gain, excitement, or success) Taking risks is essential if you want to win. Things just don't fall out of the sky and into our laps. We have to get up and do something. I understand that jumping out of the boat can be scary, but in order to get to dry land, especially if your boat was disabled, it would be the only way. People who take risks don't necessarily know the outcome yet, but their belief is so strong that there is a goal that needs to be reached. Yes, it can be scary, but what can be scarier than staying where you are the rest of your life with no growth, change, advancement or happiness?

I remember when my son and I moved to Florida from Philadelphia. I left behind a house, my entire family, my salon, and all of my clientele. People thought I was crazy, but I needed the change. I knew that it would take me a while to get on my feet again and get re-established, but I had the mindset, "You only live on this earth once, and you never know when your time will be up, so why not!" That was the best decision I could have made, because not only did I meet some great people, I was able to see my vision more clearly and work towards it.

Never allow fear to take over and keep you stuck. It would suck becoming a senior citizen and looking back and saying... I woulda, coulda, shoulda." Pray, build your faith up, surround yourself with awesome people and jump!

Have Trust (belief that someone or something is reliable, good, honest, and effective) Trust is something that is built over time. When babies start to walk, they get a little fearful of falling at first, but as they keep trying, they finally get the hang of it. And even if they still fall a few times, they are not fearful because they know that they can get right back up. Take some pointers from those precious little human beings. Everything was designed to teach us lessons in our lives. Remember that everything is steps. If things were so easy at first, then everyone would be at the top. Trust that you will make it where you need to be. There is one little secret I live by and I say to myself, "If I stay the course, be obedient, and have faith, while doing the work, I will be where I am supposed to be when I am supposed to be there." Trust me, if you can sit in a chair every day without thinking that it will collapse, then you can believe that your purpose will come to pass.

Be a Leader – (a guiding or directing head) Leadership is an amazing thing, but it comes with a price. No leader gets to where they are just because they are a good person. You have to adapt those qualities. Leaders are the ones who stay up late and put the work in to make it easier for everyone else, invent creative ideas for others, take the hit for everyone else, are smart enough to have a team of people to take some of the weight off of them so they can be more effective, and not keep everything to them-selves – they believe in themselves enough that they have no problem trusting and passing the baton as Myles Munroe would say.

You know that you are capable of leadership when you are comfortable in your own skin. That is of number one importance. I struggled with my leader-ship skills plenty of times. I remember when I ran a teen moms group from my church. I had 17 girls. Some were pregnant and the others already had a child. That was my heart and my passion. I went above and beyond to make sure these girls had a safe place to share and be themselves. We would meet at my home every Tuesday evening. We would have fun weekend trips and stay at hotels. At times, I would pick a few of them up and take them out. It was an amazing feeling for me to help these girls.

But this was also the time in my life where I was in the mental abuse relationship that I mentioned ear-lier in chapter three. I was knocked off kilter and lost focus. Also, my son started acting up in school, prob-ably because much of my attention was focused on the girls. Unconsciously, I let the girls go by the way-side, so I could deal with my own problems. Eventually, the group was cancelled and I left the girls hanging. That bothered me for years, but I learned to forgive myself and move on.

From a little girl, I possessed leadership qualities, but, of course, they had to be honed when I grew older.

Be Strategic – (of great importance within an integrated whole or to a planned effect). You have to be strategic by having a plan. You cannot operate any organization, any business, or for that matter, yourself, if you don't have a plan. When you are planning, you have to invest in time management, flexibility, and organization.

If I were to ask most people to think about what the word strategy means, most people would think of competitiveness, board games, and getting ahead. Think about a game of checkers. Whether you have the red or black pieces, the objective is to get all of your men to the opponent's side so they can be put down and you can have double power. Well, being strategic with a game plan for your vision is the same way; the only difference is you want to do it in a way where everyone wins. Don't be so bent on getting ahead that you topple over everyone else to make them lose. There is enough success to go around.

Write your vision down on paper, and then categorize the steps that it's going to take to get there. Take your time to dissect each step and work on them in order. Sometimes when doors start to open up, they will not happen in the order you planned. That's why it is important to be prepared and flexible. If not, you will be so starched on how you think it's supposed to go that you might be missing out on a blessing that is trying to happen.

Organization is also important, because if something happens out of order, you need to be able to handle it accordingly. If there is no organization, you will go crazy, get frustrated and quit, because it will become overwhelming. And lastly, time management is a must. If you burn yourself out and don't put time constraints on certain things, then you will create a disaster.

For example, if you are working on a few things at once, you have to balance your time. If they all have the same deadline and you spend more time on one, then the others will go lacking. Take these pointers and put them to good use. See you on the other side of the board!

Be Creative – (resulting from originality of thought, expression, imaginative) Dreamers are considered to be creative people. But the ones that stand out the most are the ones who actually bring that creativity to life. Bringing your creativity to life is the first step. It gives you something beyond just visualization, it gives you hands on. Being creative keeps you from being stale and getting stuck in the norm.

Creativity allows you to express a part of yourself that makes you happy. You are also more adaptable to change and have a greater tolerance for discomfort.

That's why things work out a little better in your favor. Boredom is definitely not a word in your vocabulary, because you are always thinking. As soon as you finish one thing, you are on to the next, and it's pretty easy for you to manage because you pay good attention to detail. But you need a supportive climate and sensitive environment to do so. Just know that when you are creative, your passion grows even stronger because it fuels the fire in more ways to reach your goal with different methods. Have fun with your natural God-given abilities and utilize them with all your might. You never know what may come out of it.

Exhibit Good Character – (one who believes in honesty, justice, loyalty and is one who abides by his principles) In order to reach higher heights, you have to be a person of good moral character. You have to be a person of respect, be considerate of others and tolerant. You also need to be responsible and use self-control - think before you act and consider the consequences. You are accountable for your choices and decisions—don't blame others for your actions. Responsible people try to do their best, and they persevere even when things don't go as planned. Be fair, opened minded, and listen to others. Don't take advantage of them. Play by the rules correctly, take turns and share. Don't pull a tantrum just to get your way - people are watching you. Care and compassion go a long way; when you care about others, you express gratitude, forgiveness and you help people in need. This should actually be number one on the list because you were forgiven at one point in your life, so why not extend that to someone else? This is the whole reason for your vision to come to pass, so your passion and purpose can be of good service to the world. And, lastly, please be a good citizen. If you advocate for a safe and healthy school and community, you are demonstrating good citizenship. A good citizen obeys laws and rules and respects authority. Being a good neighbor and cooperating with others are also parts of good citizenship.

Be Aggressive – (characterized by or tending toward unprovoked offensives, attacks, invasions, or the like; militantly forward or menacing) Matthew 11:12 says, "And the violent take it by force!" That should be your attitude about life. It doesn't say to be aggressive in a negative manner, but stand your ground, pull up your boot straps, bust through all barriers...and make it happen! The average person doesn't walk with this attitude 24/7 because life's issues can come and definitely beat you down, but that's when your aggression should really kick in to full gear. Take a bull, for example. I went to Cancun one year and during the trip I went to a bull fight.

Now, if you've never been to a bull fight, it is very interesting. After the preshow with all of the little pretty horses prancing around together in unison doing tricks and following orders, out came a bull with a few Matadors. I had no idea what was about to happen because this was my first time. A man on a horse came out and he had blades on his boots. After guiding the horse towards the bull, the man positioned his boots alongside the bull so it could cut the bull. After the attack, the bull went crazy! I, mean the spectators like myself who had not seen that before were in awe! The funny thing that I laugh about now is, I wanted to call the animal paramedics after I saw all the blood squirting everywhere because I was still clueless. I kept saying to myself, "Why isn't anyone doing anything about this?"

The bull's aggression was so intense from the pain that he was trying to jump the wall and get into the stands where the audience was. I need you to take a lesson from this bull. Don't give up and quit when the going gets tough, get innocently mad and take that thing by force! Understand your position!

Be Prepared – (made at an earlier time for later use: made ready in advance, ready for something: in a suitable condition for some purpose or activity) This is one of my favorites. I love being prepared. I feel like preparation is key, especially when opportunity presents itself, you need to be ready for it. There are a lot of procrastinators out there who say they want to be successful, but they are never prepared. In order to be prepared, you have to be organized with everything. Your house, your car, your personal space and your life – DE clutter. If you were to go to my mother's house, you would be amazed! Everything and anything is labeled and put away neatly. If something came up as an emergency, she would be able to put her hands on whatever is needed in a matter of seconds.

In order to get yourself prepared, follow these steps: mentally prepare, get a head start and plan to work. When I am writing a book, I am already thinking about the title of the next one. Then I go to the store and purchase my notebook to begin notes for the book. My thoughts come clearer when I physically handwrite them. After that, I create my outline, characters, lesson plans, thoughts or whatever suits the genre of the book. Then I put it on a flash drive and store it away until I am ready to start working on it. While all of this is going on, I am still working on the current book. When I am finished with that book, I submit it to the editor. Now, I am on to the next one. By the time I get to the next one, all of the extra work is done and all I have to do is relax and write. I find that the book flows easier that way.

Find what works for you when it comes to preparation. It is one of the best gifts that you could give yourself because it makes life so much easier.

Get Education – (field of study that deals with the methods and problems of teaching) Education works hand-in-hand with nearly everything we've talked about. There is not much we can do without having the knowledge to know how to do it. Therefore, learning is key to long-lasting success. Now that you've learned something, don't put it on the shelf and forget about it. It needs to be pulled back out and reviewed from time to time. You can read the same thing about 10 times and get a different revelation each time. In addition, be forever learning and don't stop. The minute you stop is the minute you lose. I know it sounds cliché', but it's true.

Have you ever been invited to a seminar by a friend who wanted you to get involved in a new business venture? They were all pumped up and providing lots of information about their product. Then suddenly you get a revelation and start getting excited but you hold back until you find out more details? Your excitement was coming from the women and men who gave their testimonies on how they were not doing so well financially, and then all of a sudden when they entered the business, they followed the easy steps that were given, and became wealthy...yadda...yadda...yadda.. Trust me, it wasn't that simple. They had to do a lot of online classes, one class with their group leader, and attend a seminar at least once a week. Now don't get me wrong there are some legitimate businesses out there that don't require as much and you actually can do well quickly, but there are very few.

The description I just gave you was all about education. Those business associates learned the art form of business structure, how to present the product properly to gather members and keep them, and how to train the members that joined their teams so they could bring new members in. The knowledge that they attained to succeed came from education. They put dedication and time in to learn how to become successful. And guess what? It's not wise to stop educating yourself after you get wealthy because if you do you will have no idea on what to do when the ever-changing procedures come about on how to keep your business growing. You will either become stagnate, or lose what you already have. Make sure that doesn't happen...Stay forever learning!

Characteristic of an Eagle

Tenacious – (take risks...take advantage of opportunities (perseverance)

Watch an eagle when a storm comes. When other birds fly away from the storm with fear, an eagle spreads its wings and uses the current to soar to greater heights. The eagle takes advantage of the very storm that lesser birds fear and head for cover. Challenges in the life of a leader are many. These are the storms we must face as leaders to rise to greater heights. Like an eagle, a leader can only rise to greater heights if he takes up the challenges head-on without running away from them. This is yet another leadership characteristic.

Activity

- ➤ Find a partner.

- ➤ Tell each other what one of your passions are along with two strengths you possess.

- ➤ Your partner will invent a 25-second story about you based on the passion and the two strengths that you told them.

- ➤ You will then take the 25-second story and personalize it and add the Eagle characteristic given in the previous page and write the story on the worksheet **"Affirm the Possibilities."**

- ➤ Now do the reverse with your partner.

- ➤ Let's discuss what you wrote, and what it will take to successfully accomplish the content in these stories.

- ➤ (You are speaking into each other's lives as well as writing your vision down.)

Affirm the Possibilities

My Story:

Chapter Five

Help! My Image is Trapped

Master the 7 basic steps in creating your personal brand and make yourself an expert in high demand

"If you do what you always did, you get what you always got."

~Anonymous~

Image:

A representation of the external form of a person or thing.

Dig Deep

➢ Close your eyes and think about three things that you could do to improve your image.

➢ Write the three things down on the **Thought Bubble Worksheet.**

➢ Write your answer underneath your three things.

(Optional) Discuss your answers

1.

2.

3.

1.

2.

3.

7 Steps to Personal Branding

Determining your unique value is just a matter of thinking about or discovering what it is you are most passionate about. Most of the time, we are operating in it and don't even recognize that we are doing so. What you have to offer is unique because it's yours and no one can take that. It doesn't matter if everyone you know is doing the same thing. If that gift was given to you, then it was meant for you to utilize. I see many people staying stagnant because they don't believe what they have to offer is good enough or unique. When you start to believe in what you do, others will follow. People watch other people to find out if they can be trusted and if they have confidence in what they are offering. When you have faith in yourself, as well as your product, and it is genuinely natural, it will spill out without you needing to try. You have to believe that no one else can do it like you can and offer what you have. Determining your unique value is simple. If you enjoy doing something without getting paid for it and you do it with ease, and people are benefiting from it......then that may be your answer.

Creating your Image is one of the most important things you could do. If you don't look like what you do, then it doesn't matter how good your product or your gift is, people won't follow you. Let's take a hairstylist, for example, if you needed your hair professionally done and treated with care, you are not going to go to a stylist who has dated hair along with dry, brittle split ends. Her image basically screams out, "I'm a mess and I really don't care about healthy, stylish hair!" Below are a few things that need to be taken care of so you can look inviting and marketable with your brand.

Skin should always be clear, smooth, and natural. If you have a severe problem with acne or you have a lot of abrasions on your body that will not go away, make sure you see a dermatologist. If it's minor annoying issues, try getting facials that offer deep cleansing, microdermabrasion, face peels, or even laser treatments. And for your body, try using Shea Butter after you get out of the shower or before you go to bed. You will be amazed at the transformation your skin will make. Again, quite often it is our diet. Don't forget to drink water, especially at night. While your body is resting and replenishing itself, the water is helping the process a little easier by flushing out toxins. This is not for everyone because it can cause several bathroom trips in the middle of the night. If you fuel your body with a lot of white sugar, sodas, saturated fats, and processed foods, then, of course, it has to exit somewhere, and most of the times it is our skin.

Hands and feet are an important part also. They should always be well manicured and pedicured. If you wear polish, make sure it's not chipped. If you get acrylic, gel, or silk-wrapped nails, make sure you get fills when it's time. Don't allow your nails to grow out and have an obvious line of demarcation. If your nails are dirty underneath, clean them. Sometimes the best thing to wear on your nails is neutral colors, clear, French or American manicures because you can get away with them a little longer than you would a brighter color nail polish.

Hair is known as the fashion plate of the world. Its presence will be known walking through the door before you. It's funny how nothing else could be put together, but if your hair is done, then you look good. It almost doesn't make sense but that's how it is viewed. Get yourself a good hairstylist that's going to care for your hair along with making it suitable for you. There's nothing worse than having a pretty style, but unhealthy hair because of the lack of proper professional care.

Makeup is a statement all in itself. I know there are women out there against wearing makeup because they prefer to be all natural. That is totally okay and I have nothing against it. I think it is absolutely awesome when I see a woman who doesn't need makeup because her skin is flawlessly glowing. But there are specific occasions that call for it. There are only a few items you need in your arsenal: foundation, concealer, blush, lipstick and lip gloss, mascara, and eye shadow.

Foundation is for coverage. It is used to even out your skin tone to give it that polished look. And if you are going to be out for a long time and you want it to last, it's good to invest in a primer which goes on your face before the foundation to keep the foundation locked in and give it a smoother finish. It's just like painting a wall. Most times, before you put the actual color paint on the wall, you lay a foundation with primer. Concealer is used for those stubborn blemishes on your face from either a blackhead or dark circles under the eyes from lack of sleep. Blush is a great enhancer just to brighten up your face, and give it a pop as well as eye shadow. Mascara makes your eyes pop with the right brand. Be careful when using some water proof brands, it can make your lashes brittle and break off. And, lastly, lipstick and gloss. These are the two most worn makeup products amongst women. There's nothing like a nice pretty lip. Make sure you have natural bristle makeup brushes. They apply smoother, are easier to wash, and last longer. Some days all you need is foundation and lip gloss, and other days you may need every item depending on the event or circumstance. One thing to remember is less is best. Always use sparingly. You never want to walk out of the house looking like a clown, especially if the lighting in your bathroom is dull. Bad personal grooming can be spotted a mile away - don't let it be you.

Dressing for Success shows that you are about your business. If your clothes are not ironed, you have a run in your stockings, dirty scuffed shoes, a weak shirt collar and a too small pair of pants then that states that you are not dressed for success. It is said that 55% of another person's perception of you is based on how you look. One source states, "75% of recruiters believe that how a person dresses for work affects their job, salary, and possible promotions." First impressions are everything. Casual attire can sometimes translate to casual work. **Try wearing a skirt suit.** This works really well in any work environment providing the skirt is not too tight. In a more casual workplace separates like skirts and colored jackets look great too. A dress and jacket also look good together. Think elegance here. Sweater dresses cut to knee length with a toning jacket is another great look for a more casual workplace. **Avoid showing cleavage.** Traditional work colors are black (chic), navy (trustworthy), red (dynamic, aggressive), grey (conservative). If you want to venture into a broader range of colors, just make sure it is appropriate to your work setting, as well as your skin tone. **Learn what your color palette' is and what styles suit you.** If you don't know use a personal stylist and find out the best colors to bring out the best in your skin tone and hair color. **Remember to make your jewelry very simple and not gaudy.** Your jewelry should not outshine you when you walk into a room. However, some large types of jewelry look good, depending on the profession that you are in, like fashion artist, makeup artist, and hair artist. Look at yourself in a long mirror before leaving the house. Make sure you invest in good quality clothes so you don't have to replace them every four to six months. Invest in a few key power outfits that will last a couple of years.

If you aspire to be successful, look as if you mean business and are a competent, confident, professional individual. Clothing sends out very powerful messages about who we are, so dress to make a positive impression. Dress as you want to be seen: Serious, professional, upward-bound and ready to meet clients. Dressing for success is a necessary component to obtaining it.

The traditional man can look good in a button-down shirt, tie, polished black shoes, blue, black or gray jacket, and slacks that complement the jacket. And we almost forgot socks. Two dozen pairs of identical black or blue dress socks are good to have.

The traditional woman looks good in a skirt that hits just above the knee, slacks and perhaps pantsuits, simple jewelry, polished flats or moderate heels. Before we end this topic, remember, your professional appearance can create credibility.

Targeting your Market is not as difficult as it sounds. Once you discover your unique value, think about who needs you, and how they can benefit from you and your product. You have to find your niche market. A niche market simply means identifying and sectioning out a particular genre of people. Let's take Mattel toys, for example. They make a large variety of children toys, and some are created for boys, girls and unisex. Now some of their most popular brands are hot wheel cars. The majority of children that play with them are boys, which Mattel intended to target. They needed to go a little deeper, so it wouldn't be so broad, so they associated the cars with an age group of 5 years and older. They uniquely and specifically made them for that group because of the smaller pieces that a younger child may put in their mouth and choke on. Okay, now we ask the question 'Why didn't they just make them bigger to satisfy the needs of all ages? Well, if they were created any bigger, they would not be as effective on the racing track because of their bulkiness. They knew that the age group of boys 5 years and over would clean those cars off of the shelves because of their rough and rugged nature.

Be different from the rest and make sure you stand out. When someone sees your personal brand or your product brand, they should not have to second guess. They should know right away if they will benefit or not.

Getting Organized does not come easy for some. The lack of organization will definitely bring on delay in any plans or projects you may be working on. In order to properly and effectively get your brand rolling and on the move, you have to make sure that you have everything in place before, during and after you get started. I want to give you a list of things to do that will help you organize yourself, as well as, help your brand to run efficiently. They are listed in order. Let's get started.

Registering your brand name begins with checking online to see if it is already in use by someone else. You can check sites like sba.gov or sunbiz.com if you live in Florida, for example. It has to be registered in the state that you will be branded or doing business. Some states do not require registration, so check and see if registration is required in your state. Also, if you are using your own legal name, you may not have to register, depending on how it's used. A term brand name is sometimes used interchangeably with DBA (doing business as), fictitious name, business name or trade name. If you are registering a DBA, you will be filing as a sole proprietor. Remember, every state has their own filing requirements, so follow instructions.

Domain name is a unique name that identifies an internet resource such as a website, for example; Candraward.com or Askcandra.com. It is really important to get a few of these, because you will need them to publish a website. There are places you can get them from like www.godaddy.com.

Tax and licenses are an important part of the branding process, especially, if you are turning yourself into a full-blown business and will be receiving money from customers and clients. First, you want to register with the IRS and get an EIN number (Employer Identification number). That is what your business will be identified with. Then you want to register with your state tax or revenue office, so you will be on file and properly taxed. You may also need to register for a sales tax permit, which allows you to legally collect sales tax from customers or clients. Next, you want to apply for the appropriate business license and permit, depending on your genre of business.

Getting Trademarked is not mandatory, but it is a decision you have to make if you want to protect your name and or logo from someone else using it. A trademark typically protects brand names and logos used on goods and services. Your company name is not necessarily a brand name -- and not all company names can get trademark protection. If it is too broad like "At Home Babysitting" the Trademark Office may consider that too basic to qualify for protection, as it merely describes what you do. Not every submitted trademark gets through. It actually takes anywhere from 4 months to a year to determine if it will pass the board or not. Remember, this is only for the US; it does not qualify for worldwide protection. There are additional steps you need to take to register your trademark in accordance with various international treaties.

Creating a Website is a very essential step to creating your brand. Websites are basically an online business card and resume. It sends a message as to who you are and what you have to offer. It is good to get your site done by a professional. If you are not able to, you can create your own website for free or pay a minimum monthly fee on Wix.com, Weebly.com, Squarespace.com and a few others. Make sure your site has a blog page, about, store, testimonial, contact, media, events or press and other content you want to share. There is really no limit on pages to have, but remember you don't want to overwhelm your viewers. No more than nine pages are effective.

Make sure to create and send out a monthly newsletter consistently to keep your followers informed. Keep in mind that you don't have to limit your topics to just your expertise, you want to break up the monotony with celebrity news, world news or just the latest fashions or sales at Macy*s. You can use a site called mail chimp to create your newsletters. When it comes to your blog, make sure that you are consistent as well. You never want to gain the reputation as not being trustworthy, so make sure to publish on time. With your blogs, you have to be true to yourself. People like real people. They want to be connected to you while you are in your bathrobe with curlers in your hair, if you know what I mean. Be You!

Business cards are great especially when you are out and about and you want to share yourself with the world. They are very inexpensive to make now, compared to years ago. The only thing you have to do is tell the company what design and layout you want and they can be printed within a matter of days. There are also free websites that allow you to create your own such as Vistaprint.com and others. Make sure your name and contact info such as your business and or personal phone number, business e-mail, website address, who you are and what you do in brief is on the card. And most importantly put your website in eyes view because the main purpose of your business card should be to lead people to your bigger business card, which is your website.

Develop a 30- Second Pitch Speech to introduce yourself and your business quick and easy. This is done to assure that you get an opportunity to sell yourself within a matter of seconds before a person leaves your presence. I really don't like to use the word sell because that sounds so impersonal and hard but that is basically what you are doing. Only use this if you only have a few seconds to make someone believe in you. When you are trying to gain long-lasting relationships with perspective clients individually, you want to do something I learned from Danni Johnson called F.O.R.M. (family, occupation, recreation and message). This is when you build a rapport and determine needs. You basically allow the person to let their guard down by asking them about their family, occupation and recreation. Then you can bring your message or your pitch. Remember, people always want to know what's in it for them (WIIFM) so don't make it all about you. They want to know that when they use your service or product they will receive the best of what you have to offer and even more.

Testimonies are more important than you may think. The first thing most people are drawn to are testimonies. They want to see how others benefited from either knowing you or purchasing a product from you. You can get testimonials from friends, clients, co-workers, and others that may have had a positive experience with you and were pleased.

Create a 60-90 second personal commercial to let people see you and get to know you up front and personal. Many people are visual and go by what they see. This way, you have an opportunity to draw people's hearts in many places at one time by sharing who you are, what you do, and how they can benefit from you. This also includes creating videos of yourself describing or demonstrating your services.

Setting Goals should be in the forefront of everything you do. Make sure as you prepare to venture out, it is followed by the goals you set or you will be overwhelmed, confused and may even want to give up. There are three categories of goals that you should write down. Keep in mind that they sometimes change as you continue to achieve them.

Short-Term Goals: The first category is short-term goals, which simply means something you want to accomplish now, whether it's today, next week, next month or next year.

Mid-Term Goals: Mid-term goals fall in between short and long. There really is no true time span.

Long-Term Goals: Long-term goals can stretch from five years and beyond. Goals are achievable. They give your life direction as well as boost your motivation and self-confidence. As I mentioned earlier, one thing that can help your goals come to life is a dream board. A dream board is a free visualization tool to help you envision your best life and keep track of your goals. You can upload an app that allows you to create a virtual dream board or you can make one the old-fashioned way and hang it on your wall so you can see it as soon as you wake up and before you go to bed. The easiest way to create a dream board is to gather pictures, quotes and sayings from magazines, printed from the Internet, newspapers and books that speak your life and inspire you. Then cut them out neatly and paste them to your board, either randomly or in order, depending on how you view it.

Then hang it up in a visual place and follow your dreams.

Networking is simply involving yourself with other people online. It is socializing with others to get to know someone and getting yourself known. Social Media in this 21st century seems to be the largest form of networking outside of attending events. There are many sites to choose from, but the most popular are: Facebook, YouTube, Twitter, LinkedIn, Pinterest, Google, Tumblr, Instagram, Flicker, Vine and Meet-up. These sites are very useful for brand awareness, word of mouth advertising, increased customer loyalty and trust, and improved audience reach and influence. A great way to get followers quickly is to join groups and online communities and give feedback anytime you can.

Involve yourself in discussions that you would not normally talk about. Get involved in what's going on now and present yourself as an expert. You have to make your presence known so that people see that you are interested as well as interesting. People want to feel as if they know you personally. You want to market your personality.

Another awesome way to involve yourself online is to participate in forums and others blogs. Subscribe to the blogs in your field. You can comment on topics, become a guest blogger and share other blogs on your site. Be creative, but, most of all, be yourself and watch your list grow.

Getting Out - Attend Networking Events, accept invitations to parties, attend shows, educational classes, job functions, sports games, go to the mall, your child's school or even the college cafeteria. These are great examples of getting out and meeting people. Remember, networking is NOT just socialization with other people. You can do that standing in the grocery line. The point is to utilize every opportunity that comes your way. Always make sure to have your business cards on you to hand out. Try and hand out no less than 10 cards per day. When it comes to networking events, they are set up for a specific purpose – for people to come and interact with other like-minded people and possibly make a connection. The goal at the end of the night is for you to have handed out all of the business cards and to have collected nearly everyone's card in the room that you came across along with F.O.R.M.-ing people and using your pitch speech. Remember to try and use all forms of social media and networking and watch your brand grow beyond your imagination.

Become an Expert in your field and watch your brand take off. It's really simple to do. Keep in mind that people always want to follow something or someone they can learn from. What they look for is confidence in the expert, and the most relevant and up-to-date information. There are many ways

to help yourself gain knowledge to become and look like an expert in your field. **Reading** is one. Make sure you add reading as a must in your daily life. Try to read a book a month if you can, and don't just read, but study what you read. Be informed. **Research** things you don't know, or things that most people want to know about. Online and the library are great resources. **Take classes** to boost your knowledge in your field. Check the paper or look online for classes that may be offered, not just locally, but regionally. **Write a book** or publish articles in magazines or the newspaper.

When people see that you have taken the time to write something, it gives you a position of power in a sense that you are interested and you know what you are talking about. Traveling also gives you the advantage over some because you may have seen and experienced things that they haven't and you are able to share. Be dependable, consistent and stay fresh and relevant. Create a product or service. Do podcast, workshops, seminars, and online trainings, make DVDs, and create videos. Teach and Speak. Everyone looks up to people who can stand in front of them and help them with something that they want to know more about. It also makes you look confident and like a true expert. Stay fresh and relevant and keep your eyes on your goals. If you put these practices into play and work them correctly, you will not be disappointed.

Marketing to your Market is just summing up what we have already gone over in the previous steps. I am going to keep this really simple for you. There are no tricks, no 10-hour classes and no business degrees needed to market to your market. All you have to do is follow the F.O.R.M. formula: learn your pitch speech, become an expert and believe in yourself and your product. People don't realize that belief and confidence does all of the work. People could care less about all of the preliminaries. They just want to know if it works and how could it benefit them. Remember to use the F.O.R.M. method and don't shove yourself, your service or your product down someone's throat. The more sincere salesperson that genuinely cares about his customer and has knowledge of the product or service he is selling, always does better than the one who has no concern. Don't be the person who is more concerned with how many sales he can make that day.

Direct and Indirect marketing. Let me explain the difference between direct and indirect marketing. Direct marketing is when you communicate the value of the service or product straight forward and directly. This happens by interrupting potential customers with advertisements, cold calls, stopping them and telling them about your product whether they asked or not. Basically, you go and get them! Indirect marketing, on the other hand, is totally opposite. It's when you communicate the service or product's value indirectly by allowing the customer to come to you. This is done by creating and curating content and an atmosphere that is meaningful to them. With indirect marketing, you wear buttons and t-shirts with your brand on them to create curiosity within the potential customer where it either forces them to ask you what it means or look you up when they get home. This approach encourages the customer to put their guard down when making a decision. Remember, customers and clients prefer to purchase from courteous, knowledgeable salespeople who are passionate about their product. Your goal is to build a relationship and turn them into a repeat customer. Walk away with this in mind; own it, declare it, share it, prove it, and sell it.

Goals:

➢ Write a goal on the "My Goal" worksheet.

➢ Then write three obstacles that keep you from achieving it.

➢ Underneath that, write three things that you can do to overcome the obstacles.

My Goal Worksheet

Goal...

1.

2.

3.

                  1.

                  2.

                  3.

Characteristic of an Eagle

Vision – (focus and clarity and discipline)

If you ever happen to see an eagle sitting high above the tree or the cliff of a mountain, watch closely and see how attentive the bird is. The body sits still and the head will be tilted side-to-side to observe what is happening below, around and above it. Even if it's flying close by, you can observe how keen its eyes are looking for its prey. Eagles have a keen vision. Their eyes are specially designed for long distance focus and clarity. They can spot another eagle soaring from 50 miles away.

 Just like the eagle, all leaders must have vision. The eagle's eyes can see great distances. They can also go directly into the sun without being blinded. You, being the leader of your network marketing team, must have vision. You must have a vision that guides and leads your team towards the organization's goals. The vision must be big and focused. A big, focused vision will produce big results.

Activity:

> ➤ Effective Communication will be demonstrated in a role play activity "**It's Me**" that involves four attendees' exhibiting a correct and incorrect scenario with the four principles: Talk less and listen more, remain objective, believe in yourself and respond instead of reacting.

> ➤ Attendees' will be asked to come to the front of the room. Each attendee will be given an index card with one principle on one side and a scenario concerning the principle on the other side.

> ➤ Attendees' have to role play and act out the scenario while exhibiting the principle incorrectly on the other side of the card.

> ➤ Attendee will then reverse and act out the same scenario correctly while exhibiting the principle on the other side of the index card.

> ➤ Discussion will take place in-between each scenario.

Chapter Six

I'm ready for this thing called Life

Develop and execute the 3 P's of life skills that will help to change your life and get you to the top

"Opportunity is always missed because it is dressed up in overalls and looks like work."

~Thomas Edison~

Life Skills:

Skills that are desirable and needed for full participation in everyday life.

Dig Deep

> ➢ Close your eyes and think about three things that you could do to gain life skills.

> ➢ Write the three things down on the **Thought Bubble Worksheet.**

> ➢ Write your answer underneath your three things.

(Optional) Discuss your answers.

1.

2.

3.

1.

2.

3.

Three main categories of Life Skills:

Personal Development Skills

Integrity is a concept of consistency of actions, values, methods, measures, principles, expectations, and morals. Integrity is a personal choice and is regarded by many people as the honesty and truthfulness of one's actions. People should be able to count on you, especially when you say you are going to do something. Your integrity should never have to be second-guessed. If you live a double life and your morals change, whenever it is convenient, then you will not appear trustworthy. Your character will be challenged and it will be difficult to regain any form of reputation. People gravitate to someone or something that has great value. They like to know that wherever they focus their time or money, winning benefits will follow. If there is any lack in your life pertaining to this matter, acknowledging where you are, removing the pride and practicing to becoming better, is essential. Don't allow yourself to become defeated if you fail to achieve results in the time you may have set for yourself. Remember practice is patience and things don't happen overnight unless it is a miracle.

Responsibility is a duty or task that you are required or expected to do. It is a commitment that is taken on and executed with your family, bills, God, your community and work. It is the state of being that you are in that will cause something to happen. When I think of responsibility, I think of consistency. I became responsible when I turned 16 years of age with a newborn baby. I actually had a choice. I could have tried to force my child on my mother and do the bare minimum to take care of him, or I could have taken full responsibility by giving him affection and love, changing diapers, feeding and clothing him and financially providing the best I could, which I did. Responsibility is a very essential life skill that needs to be honed and put into practice. I know quite a few adults who still struggle in this area and want to do better, and then some who could care less. Real responsibility is for the strong-at-heart. Understand that if you want things to move in your life, then you have to get up and stop passing your responsibility off to others. If you are at work and your boss assigns something for you to do and you simply just don't feel like it, don't neglect it or ask another co-worker to do it for you.   That will put you in a position of non-trust and non-reliable. So when raise time comes you will not be a candidate. This example does not only apply to a job, it applies to every aspect of your life. Keep in mind that everything you do or don't do reflects your character and determines the status of your success.

Productivity is the state of being able to generate, create, enhance or bring forth goods and services. Productivity is essential if you expect new things to come into your life. It's a little difficult to grow your business if you are not consistent and self-motivated to get up every day on time, do research on the latest trends and techniques, network and meet other like-minded people in your field, and set achievable goals and stick to them. Remember, my friend, things will not fall from the sky. You have to actually go and get them. Being productive does not have to be a chore, it can be really fun. I find it very rewarding when I write down a list for the day or even the week and I get it accomplished. That puts me a step ahead, so when something else comes along, I won't be stifled in getting it done because of other things holding me back. There are people who want to be productive, but have no clue where to start. Well, here are a few tips that will help you.

Write down what you want to accomplish in order. Organization is key, because it helps you to delegate what is most important and what would be more beneficial. After writing your list, allot yourself a specific time to get it done. Once you are done, start on the next. Don't allow yourself to sit down after that list and think that's it. Too many times people get comfortable with old accomplishments and sit back and marvel over what they did, which is past tense. Remember the world is still moving.

Lastly, revisit and analyze what you could do better to grow. Keep in mind, there will always be time for a break, but things need to be in order so when it is time for you to relax, you will have no worries of stagnation.

Problem Solving is a mental process that involves discovering, analyzing and working through details of a problem to reach a solution. It's a complex cognitive process where people identify problems and develop methods for resolving them. Problem solving should be taught from pre-school age. It is key to how a child, and ultimately an adult, respond to real-life situations. People who possess this skill have better control over their lives and are able to cope with challenges that come their way. Interpersonal and personal relationships fail because of poor problem-solving. Problem solving can come in many forms and degrees, from what color shoes you are going to wear to whether or not you should sign that contract. It doesn't matter how mundane or how complex a problem is, you still have to use the same cognitive skill to reach a solution. When you reach an understanding that all you have to do is just weigh the options and make a simple choice, then you will have peace in whatever decision you make. Remember that it is not that serious. Life is what you make it, so please keep it simple.

Time Management is the act or process of planning and exercising conscious control over the amount of time spent on specific activities, especially to increase effectiveness, efficiency and productivity. It is something that so many people struggle with. It can be the detriment to becoming successful in your endeavors. Many good, deserving people have great ideas and contribute excellent gifts and talents that deserve Grammy and Emmy awards, but the one thing that can kill and destroy a dream is the lack of time management. The way to overcome this problem is first to acknowledge it.

Secondly, you have to sit down and write everything that causes this behavior in your life. Whether it's the fact that you just love to sleep late, don't prepare yourself the night before with ironing your clothes, making your lunch, getting the kids together, or simply just don't go to bed in a timely manner, all of these things are organized based. There are other instances where some people actually do everything right, but when it's time to leave the house they can't find their keys or they don't allow enough time for traffic, which causes them to be late.

Lastly, I want to talk about the spirit of procrastination. This is a biggie and the major reason for the lack of time management. Let's take college kids, for example. Many of them wait until the last minute to get an assignment done because they don't feel like getting it out of the way in the beginning. Most of the time, their excuses are they work better under pressure. That may work for a while, but as time goes on and careers start to blossom, behaviors have to change. When other everyday life responsibilities are added to their list, waiting until the last minute will not work anymore, and it can make them ineffective. To avoid procrastination and become a person with effective time management, make sure everything you do has some kind of value. If you believe in something and you know that it will ultimately change your life, why not be on time for it?

Money Management is a process of budgeting, saving, investing, spending or overseeing the cash usage of an individual or group. Budgeting can be very difficult for some. As soon as money gets into their hands, it's gone. Many things like the lack of knowledge, no positive financial role model and living beyond your means after a decrease in income of any sort are a few of the main causes for the lack of being able to manage your money. I considered myself pretty good at handling my finances at a young age. I remember getting my allowance as well as the money I received from doing hair in my bedroom and saving it accordingly. I never splurged out of control. I didn't enjoy that feeling of being broke and having to wait around for the next opportunity of pay day. By the time I was 18, I was able to buy my own car with cash, and by the age of 19, I was able to get my first apartment for my son and I. I appreciated the gift I was given with hair because it afforded me the opportunity to live a pretty decent life as a single parent. In that industry, it can get really tricky trying to hold onto money, because hundreds of dollars are passing through your hands on a daily basis and temptation to spend can become an issue. But, because of my goals, I maintained discipline to disburse my money correctly. I had no choice but to be responsible because by age 19, I had a car note, rent, utility bills, insurance, grocery bills, and most of all, a high daycare cost. My disciplined habits followed me throughout life and made it easy to manage my finances.

People Development Skills

Communication is the act or process of using words, sounds, signs, or behaviors to express or exchange information to express your ideas, thoughts and feelings. Communication is crucial if you want to have healthy relationships with people. That is the only way you are going to get another person to understand you, as well as you understanding the other person. You can communicate verbally and non-verbally. Verbal communication is simple, you can talk and be heard. Non-verbal can be done by body language and listening. Healthy communication is dialect being shared between two or more people having a voice and fairly being heard. If you want to quickly see a friendship, relationship or even a business go down the drain, then don't communicate.

Some people are introverts by nature and don't really fall into the expressive category, but there are still ways for them to communicate effectively. For example they can e-mail, text, write letters or simply do it the old fashioned way and meet one-on-one in a peaceful environment and open up. The problem with that is, if they are talking with an extrovert, the extrovert has to learn how to allow someone else to speak and not interrupt, which is part of their nature because, for the most part, they are always excited.

Negotiating is a give-and-take process between two or more parties who each have their own aim and viewpoints. They should be seeking to discover a common ground and reach an agreement to settle a matter of mutual concern. Negotiating can be complex, especially if you are a person who likes to be in control. Controlling people don't like to give up ownership of anything, so they are never really willing to bargain. It's either their way or no way. When negotiating, you have to let your guard down and be willing to see the person's viewpoint. No one can make it successfully in this life by themselves - you need other people. You have to get out of that "It's either my way or the highway!" mentality. Whether you are dealing with the CEO of a large company or a small child, negotiating is key to a healthy and friendly environment. If you had a house on the market for $200,000 for an entire year and it was only worth $150,000 and offers were coming in for less; but you won't budge and drop because that's what you demand, then guess who loses. In the end, learn that negotiating is a good thing and if utilized in your life, it can get you very far.

Assertiveness is the quality of being self-assured and confident without negative aggression. It is a learnable skill and mode of communication and a form of behavior declared or affirmed without the need of proof. In this life, assertiveness is needed. The days of being passive and just letting anything fly, even if you don't agree, is gone. Assertiveness is standing for what you want and not taking no for an answer in a healthy and conservative manner. It is also based on balance. What makes assertiveness different from negative aggressiveness is the fact that you are still considering the rights and needs of others.

With negative aggressive behavior you take what you want regardless, and don't usually ask, which is sometimes needed in certain circumstances. Let's take a parent and their child, for example; if their child was getting bullied at school and the teacher knew, but wasn't doing anything about it and the parent found out, an aggressive parent wouldn't just give the school a call and be assertive. They would come to the school and go to the classroom and the principal's office demanding answers and possibly causing a scene if their concerns aren't satisfied.

With that being said, make sure to distinguish the difference between the two, so you know when to use them. When dealing with people, especially if it's not a serious situation, then make sure to only exhibit assertiveness. You never want to damage a good relationship whether it's family, co-worker, boss, friend or your other half over an emotion that could have been avoided with a little self-control. Remember, aggressiveness does not only come in a negative form; you just have to know when to use it.

Accountability is an obligation or willingness to accept responsibility or to account for one's actions. Everyone should have someone who they are accountable to and someone they are accountable for. It is so important to allow that into your life, because we are all human beings. No one is perfect, so a little help goes a long way. When being accountable, you have to let your guard down – that shows your humility. It's easy to hide your true self from people, but real strength comes when you can be honest. Accountability covers so many other facets. You must be accountable on your job, in school, at home, and with God. If you are just going through life and doing anything you want, whether right or wrong, without thinking of any consequences, then you are in a dangerous place. I find that people who have mentors, friends and family members who have their best interest at heart and will let them know when they are going left when they should be going right are better off in life and have higher success rates. Being accountable doesn't make you a weak individual and less of a person. It simply means that it will be easier for you to hit your goals and dreams.

Good Judgment means discernment and discretion, the ability to judge and make a decision or form an opinion objectively, authoritatively and wisely. I cannot say enough about the importance of having good judgment. I have seen so many people hit rock bottom because they trusted the wrong person or situation. I am not saying that you have to walk around staring at people as if they had some sort of disease, but you definitely need to pay attention to details when new people enter your life. If you are good at feeling people out, then you should know by the first encounter if there will be a second one. Normally, someone's aura will show before they even open their mouth to speak.

One thing I don't want you to do is size them up and have harsh judgment, as if they were on the witness stand, because sometimes our judgments can be distorted. We can sometimes be so busy trying to find something wrong that we miss out on a good person that may be meant to come into our lives to be an asset. A good way to see where someone's motives are is in their speech and in their tone. Let them do most of the talking while you just sit back, listen and chime in every now and then. For the most part, what you really need to hear will eventually come out. If there is a situation where they may not do much of the talking and you end up doing it to fill the void, then check that out also. It could be an instance where they are either feeling you out, or they don't really want you to know anything about them. In either case, always be alert and guard your heart from anything and anyone who is not supposed to have a space there.

Social Awareness involves learning about the dynamics of social relationships between individuals, groups and communities. A socially aware individual values human rights and acknowledges the importance of harmonious social interaction for the developmental progress of human beings. It is important to become socially aware because you need to understand your surroundings and what people's needs are. There are a lot of activists talking about social awareness because they are for the people, causes and change. When you become socially aware, you step out of your comfort zone into unfamiliar groups; you examine your role in conflict and have the ability to relate. You should be able to consider other's needs with empathy and compassion and not judgment. The best part about it all is that you will be able to bloom anywhere you're planted, because you have a good understanding of people and what to expect. If you have children in your life of any sort, make sure to help them become socially aware and that will guarantee them a well-balance in any situation they are put in.

Professional Development Skills

Cognitive skills are a set of abilities that are learned to varying degrees as a person grows and develops mentally. These skills should already be foundations from your youth, but not everyone moves at the same pace. If you find yourself or even know someone in the predicament of needing to work on their essential cognitive skills, then seek help or discipline your mind to focus and practice them every opportunity you get.

The first one we will talk about is **attention skills** which there are three types: *Sustained, Selective* and *Divided*. Sustained attention is the ability to stay focused and on-task for a period of time. Selective attention is the ability to quickly sort through incoming information and stay focused on one thing in spite of distractions and divided attention. It is the ability to multi-task. Unfortunately, the one that gets the most popularity is divided attention, especially in the school system where many children are being diagnosed with attention disorders. Boys are actually diagnosed more than girls.

Processing Speed is another one. This is the speed at which your brain processes information. This is where you see people taking a long time to catch on, and they may have to read something at least three times until they get it. This is because when you read, you need to be able to identify the individual and blended sounds that make each word unique.

Auditory Processing is the ability to analyze, blend and segment sounds. It's also known as phonemic awareness. Surprisingly, auditory processing is crucial not just for speaking, but also for reading and spelling. This is because when you read, you need to be able to identify the individual and blended sounds that make each word unique and recognizable.

Visual Processing is the ability to perceive, analyze and think in visual images. Visual processing is imperative for reading, remembering, walking, driving, and playing sports and literally thousands of other tasks you do every day.

Career Management is the combination of structured planning and the active management choice of one's own professional career. The outcome of successful career management should include personal fulfillment, work and life balance, goal achievement and financial security. When you manage your career without allowing your career to manage you, it gives you freedom in the choices you coherently make. You should always have a written and mapped out plan of goals that will help you along the way in your career.

Make sure you know why you want a particular job or are already working at it and how it is going to benefit you in the future. If you know that you are somewhere that has no potential for growth, then you have to come to the realization that you cannot stay there, especially if you have dreams and goals to do better. Career management also involves patience. You have to know when to make moves and not make emotional decisions. This doesn't only pertain to careers that have no growth; it also pertains to good-paying jobs with great promises.

Just because it seems like the perfect match for you and all of the qualifications line up, doesn't mean you are supposed to be a part of the company. There are specific places we need to be at specific times in our lives and we have to use discernment and pray about where we are supposed to be. I have a friend who started working at a college as a director. The position offered her full benefits, paid vacation, a steady paycheck, as well as bonuses. After being in the job for a year, she was miserable. She said that was the worst decision she had ever made. Her stress level was so high that she had to go to the emergency room for high blood pressure. After she finally resigned, her blood pressure went down instantly without medication. Now she is back doing what she was doing before she took the job which allows her to be freer in her decision-making and does not bring stress.

Self-management is the act or manner of handling direction, or control of oneself. When you possess the skill of self-management, you don't have to be micromanaged in any area of your life. Self-management puts you in the driver's seat. It supports and encourages people to access information and to develop skills that will enable them to live their lives on their terms. It is a wonderful thing when you can trust yourself and be trusted by others because of your ability to have control of your life. That makes people gravitate to you and want to know how you do what you do.

Self-management is formed from confidence and security. You can label a plethora entrepreneur's self-managers because they are their own boss. They determine when they wake, when they go into the office, when they leave and when they want to take a vacation. There is nothing wrong with working for someone else if that is your choice, but depending on your company, your freedom can sometimes be limited. So if you are a free-spirited person, make sure your employment matches your personality and needs. If not, that can cause resentment with yourself and with your employment.

Education is a form of learning in which the knowledge, skills, and habits of a group of people are transferred from one generation to the next through teaching, training, and research. I cannot stress how important education is, and I am not just talking about sitting in a classroom. I am talking about everyday learning, whether it be through the internet, reading books, going to continuing education classes and communicating with other people. I knew of someone who couldn't read and was well-educated in the area they needed to be to become successful. I know that it is hard to understand how that could be, but they knew what they wanted and they surrounded themselves with things and people they could learn from and get help. I am not advocating that you don't need to know how to read; because that is one of the most important assets a person needs to have. But what I am saying is, if you seek out ways to educate yourself, then you are already ahead of the game.

Transferable skills are aptitude and knowledge acquired skills through personal experiences such as schooling, jobs, hobbies and gifting's. Everyone should have a certain degree of transferable skills. When looking for employment, it is important to be marketable. In today's workplace, employers seek out potential employees who have multiple skills. They want to know that if they are in a crunch and have specific deadlines or are short staffed, you can pick up the slack. Transferable skills are also important to have just in case you need to find new employment. Without much job security these days, it's good to know that you are well equipped and confident enough to apply for a position that calls for requirements you are familiar with. Learn as much as you can at your job or in your business and hone those skills. Pay attention to every detail that comes your way. Study your boss as well as your co-workers. Make yourself valuable and a great asset, so that wherever you go, you will be in high demand.

Flexibility is adjusting your schedule or making significant changes to accommodate one or more person's individual needs. Flexibility involves compromise. There is no way to get ahead without being flexible. I don't care what it may pertain to in this life, if you cannot bend when a turn comes, then you will break. Trust me, if you have a hard time adjusting to change and you have to stick to the book by the letter, you will find yourself in more stressful situations than needed. Understand that circumstances and situations arise when you least expect them and you have to be flexible enough to ride along with them. There are some things that we just have no control over, which lead us to relax and be patient until it runs its course. In business, much opposition will come. You may have placed an order for a shipment that you needed to arrive at a certain time and it arrives three days later. Or you may be on your way to work and your tire blows out on the road. Now what? Do you rant and rave and send your blood pressure up higher, or do you take a deep breath, call AAA and make other arrangements with your clients or your boss? If you are responsible for a project at work and one of your team members suggests a better idea, are you going to allow pride to stand in the way and ignore their request because you believe your way is better? Or are you going to be flexible enough to try their way so the entire team can benefit? Just remember, whatever you put out, it will always return double, so make sure you choose the route that benefits you and everyone around you in the long run.

Goals:

> ➤ Write a goal on the "My Goal" worksheet.

> ➤ Then write three obstacles that keep you from achieving that goal.

> ➤ Underneath that, write three things that you can do to overcome the obstacles.

My Goal Worksheet

Goal...

1.

2.

3.

1.

2.

3.

Characteristic of an Eagle

Fearless – (face problems head on, never surrender, confidence and ambitious)

This goes back to having no fear. When you take on the characteristics of an eagle, you will learn that fear does not exist in their being, at all. I remember watching a video of an eagle ready to get dinner. There was a goat on the mountain with his herd, just minding his business. Well the eagle didn't care about the others, he was focused on that one and never feared that the others might gang up on him. He swooped down to grab the goat and missed a few times. Then the goat's herd noticed what was happening and started to run towards the eagle to protect their friend. All the eagle did was move to safety, so they couldn't get to him, but he never took his eye off of that particular goat. He gathered himself together and mapped out a strategic plan on how he was going to swoop in and ditch and dodge the other goats. Then, out of nowhere, he left his post and glided out with his slow flying and grabbed the goat while he was running. This goat was pretty big and the eagle flew into the air with him and carried him over the mountains while he was looking for a place of solitude to eat him. I watched that video several times because it was amazing. What I learned was, regardless of the giants who are bigger than you, all it takes is no fear, a will to conquer, and healthy aggression. Just like David and Goliath.

Activity:

➢ This activity is called **Charades**.

➢ Everyone will receive an index card that cannot be viewed until instructed.

➢ If there are more than four people then two teams can be created.

➢ The runner up will draw a piece of paper out of a hat or box or bag.

➢ Each card will have a word on it pertaining to a life skill, and it will have to be acted out non-verbally.

➢ The runner up's team mates will have 90 seconds to guess what the word is while the opposing team has to be silent.

➢ The winners will receive a prize.

About the Author

Candra Ward is an ambitious catalyst who is fueled with passion and drive when it comes to life transformation. She has spent over seventeen years' acquiring special skill sets that have allowed her to touch as many lives as she has.

Her journey began in 1996 when she decided to dedicate her time to mentor the youth. She had a burning desire to help others. Her faith, zeal and drive for life were what gravitated her to them. Candra was then given an opportunity to impart wisdom and life into women who were imprisoned. Her high impact and interactive workshops and seminars are life transforming and memorable. She points people in the right direction on their road to success.

Candra has facilitated workshops and seminars on; Leadership, life skills, passion and purpose, self-esteem, teen parenthood, entrepreneurship, beauty and more.

As a former at risk teen, 15 year old pregnant mother, and an emotionally struggling adult, Candra knew what it was like to suffer from dysfunctions. Her resilience to bounce back to normalcy and victory has created a pathway for her to help others become conquerors of their lives. She uses her own compelling story of adversity and triumph to show that regardless of where you may have come from or what your personal challenges may be, anything is possible if you are willing to get out of your own way. Her life of faith and endurance proves that success in life is about making the right choices and being willing to overcome the inevitable obstacles.

Candra is a Philadelphia native and now resides in South Florida with her husband and two sons. After 22 years in the beauty industry, 10 years of salon ownership and two years as a licensed educator in Cosmetology, she became a stay at home mom and is now currently in the process of completing her fifth book, hair product line and Hair Speaks Academy which will serve beauty industry professionals with education. Sometime soon in the near future Candra will be opening her *first non- profit organization for troubled youth and teenage mothers.*

"My hopes are to see everyone empowered to take control over their lives and share what they have with the next generation."

Additional copies of this book can be purchased from www.askcandra.com, Rain Publishing and online bookstores.
www.rainpublishing.com

R RAIN PUBLISHING

Books by Candra Ward

A TROUBLED GIRL'S JOURNEY INTO FREEDOM

In My Mind
CANDRA WARD
A Memoir

CAUGHT UP!
CANDRA WARD

21 Things Your Hairstylist Should Tell You
Ask Candra
CANDRA WARD

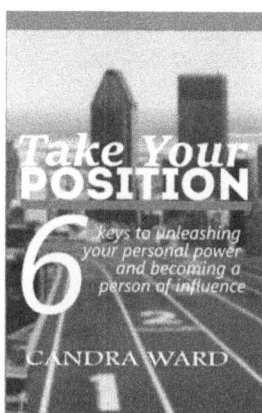

Take Your POSITION
6 keys to unleashing your personal power and becoming a person of influence
CANDRA WARD

Candra Ward
The 90 Day Devotional for Hairstylists
Challenge yourself to becoming a better You

www.ingramcontent.com/pod-product-compliance
Lightning Source LLC
Chambersburg PA
CBHW061721020426
42331CB00006B/1032